Reflections
from a
Mother's Heart

GLADYS MARIE CURRAN KEHR

Order this book online at www.trafford.com
or email orders@trafford.com

Most Trafford titles are also available at major online book retailers.

Printed in the United States of America.

ISBN: 978-1-4269-9341-1 (sc)
ISBN: 978-1-4269-9342-8 (e)

Trafford rev. 02/27/2012

 www.trafford.com

North America & international
toll-free: 1 888 232 4444 (USA & Canada)
phone: 250 383 6864 ♦ fax: 812 355 4082

Dedicated to
Gladys and Pat
The Siamese Twins

because
for the first five years
of my life,
I thought that was my name.

Personal Portrait

Your full given name	**Gladys Marie Curran**
Your Date of Birth	**April 13, 1930**
Your place of Birth	**Pottstown, PA**
Your mother's full name	**Berniece Lillie Hendrickson**
The place and date of her birth	**Camden, New Jersey—April 17, 1908**
Your father's full name	**Laurence Leo Curran**
The place and date of his birth	**Chester, Pennsylvania—May 14, 1905**
The names of your paternal grandparents	**Rose Carroll and James Curran**
The places and dates of their birth	**Felton, PA July 9, 1874 and Rathdowney, Ireland June 25, 1871**
The names of your maternal grandparents	**Emma Ludwick and Elwood Hendrickson**
The places and dates of their birth	**Salem, NJ October 12, 1884 and Pottstown, PA Mar 17, 1878**

The names of your siblings	<u>Patricia, Jane, Laurence, James, Thomas, Ruth, and Michael</u>
The places and dates of their births	<u>Patricia, Pottstown, PA June 30, 1931; Jane Camden, NJ September 10, 1934; Laurence Camden, NJ August 31, 1936; James Honolulu, TH October 27, 1941; Thomas Long Beach, CA November 22, 1946; Ruth Long Beach, CA October 13, 1948 and Michael Long Beach, CA February 16, 1950.</u>
The date and place of your marriage	<u>May 18, 1950 Long Beach, California</u>
The full given name of your husband	<u>Kenneth Clifford Kehr</u>
The names and birthdates of your children	<u>Judaline Anna, September 26, 1948; Doris March 14, 1951; Lisa June 14, 1957; Jane September 18, 1959; Kenneth October 26, 1960; John September 11, 1964; Michele April 4, 1966; Elaine May 19, 1967</u>

What is your favorite?

Flower	**Lilac**	*Bible Verse*	
Perfume	**Lilac**	*Dessert*	**Bread Pudding and Whiskey Sauce**
Color	**Green**	*Vacaion Spot*	**A Mountain Lake**
Hymn or Song	**Morning Has Broken**	*Type of food*	**Meat and Vegetables**
Book		*Sport*	
Author		*Leisure Activity*	

When did you first go to church? What are your earliest memories of the church?

I was about two and a half years old, in the town of Haddonfield, NJ. I could probably still find someone who will say, "I remember your father walking you and your sister to the front pew of Christ the King when you were only toddlers." I was interested in the celebrant and his gestures towards the congregation to the point of mimicking all of his actions until Daddy put a stop to my playacting. I loved the pageantry of the various liturgical celebrations and the melodic rhythm of the Gregorian chant always sounds to me like a cradle song. The colors in the vestments of the priest, in the stained glass windows and in the trappings of the altar and the flickering vigil lights were in sharp contrast to the austerities of everyday life. I was particularly impressed by processions and I prided myself on my ability to stay directly in back of the person in front of me and exactly the space of a pew separating us. I didn't like wearing a white dress and long white stockings and a veil or kneeling on cold marble floors. But in the spring with the aroma of roses and sweet peas, it was a beautiful sight. I always felt that God, Who was beyond such human expressions, was present in our midst as our Father with his children.

What was your favorite subject in grade school, junior high school, and high school? What was your major in college? Why?

History and literature, probably because I was steeped in both by Mother and Dad. From the time I was three years old, I was taught history. Daddy had a picture of the Cabinet of F.D.R., who was the President. He taught me to name each person in that picture and to pick each one out as he named them. Both Daddy and Mother knew history well. My Mother had a talent for remembering even obscure figures from the past. Daddy never missed an opportunity to show us an historical site or to tell us all the details surrounding it. I remember Daddy taking Pat and me with him to see New York City and my parents were enthusiastic tourists covering Washington, D.C. on foot and explaining the sights to us. Mother and Daddy were avid readers and they had at their command an impressive treasury of poetry which they would share with us. Daddy could recite all of Paul Revere's Ride, The Charge of the Light Brigade, Preparedness and other more romantic verses. Mother's taste was shown in poems such as Abou Ben Adhem, Trees or the poems of Robert Louis Stevenson, James Whitcomb Riley and John Greenleaf Whittier.

How old were you when you understood that God loves you? Recall your early thoughts about God's love.

My first thoughts about God involved my curiosity about life. A major preoccupation concerned what God would do about all the human goods left behind when we all died. It seemed such a waste if God intended to destroy so many beautiful and useful material things. I knew that God could do all things that He was all powerful, but His power impressed me less than His presence, His all seeing, and all knowing presence. He knew all sides of a dispute, the abilities and weaknesses and strength of each one of us. I always felt justified in the sense that God knew me and that He recognized my goodness or my wanting Reality even with my poor performance. I was only a little child in a society of powerful authority figures. I respected authority, but seeing the need for authority figures, I could see early on that there were alternate ways of leading others. I never had a fearful image of God laying down the law or lying in wait for me to screw up so that He could punish me. I always felt that God was on my side, caring for me and encouraging me and that He would prevail. Then everyone would know the Truth.

Did you learn to swim? How?

I have always loved the water and I find no other environment so all-encompassing, comfortable and compatible with my physical needs. Of course, this may stem from my sensitivity to temperature and the fact that the symptoms of exposure to extremes are most speedily eased by submersion in hot or cold water. My first memories of water are my daily bath in the bathroom tub or the oval enamel tub set on the kitchen table near the woodstove. The first time that I remember being in a swimming pool, I was about three years old and my mother had stripped me down to my panties so that I could bathe at Mountwell Park. In Hawaii we went in the water every day. At ten I told my parents that the secret of learning to swim was to keep one foot on the ground. I kept on swimming, the most delightful relief from the fearsome heat in Wildwood, NJ and in Santa Cruz, CA, until I could swim and float and even dive. I sometimes had the advantage of an instructor, but mostly it was trial and error. I can swim, but I cannot vouch for my form or grace as I made my way through the water.

Do you remember your first communion? What influence did it have on you and your family?

Only vaguely since unbeknownst to my parents or myself, I was on the verge of breaking out with another strain of measles. So I remember the Church and my going through the motions, but little else. I do remember the preparations. The importance of the occasion impressed me more because of my Daddy's seeing my First Holy Communion Day as the happiest day of my life. Mother and Daddy gave me a beautiful white prayer book and rosary. The prayer book had a hard shiny celluloid cover with a crucifix inset in the inside cover. The downside of the day was not the measles but the costume that was required. I don't think that I ever saw a child in this era dressed in a manner that would have been considered indecent in any sense, but there was great emphasis on every detail of our attire. According to the precise directions of the Sisters (as if my parents needed instructions) I wore a white net dress with detachable sleeves (sleeves required) and a wide net collar bordered with satin ribbon. The veil was tulle with a cap formed by elastic that fit around the head and it covered all of one's hair. The white cotton stockings and shoes completed the outfit. Ugh! Not me! I heartily dislike white.

Did you learn to sew or make other crafts? How and when? What was the first thing you made?

Crocheting was a common pastime when I was a child. Handkerchiefs were edged with lacy crocheted borders. I remember being sent to the notions store to have a piece of material prepared with a picot edge (small holes on the edge of cloth so that one could attach the crocheted border). Embroidering was another popular craft, but I crocheted more often because everything I needed was usually on hand. Mother and Mommom crocheted everything from edges and doilies to dresses, baby things, tablecloths, and bedspreads. I stuck to handkerchiefs. In high school I began knitting and one of the Sisters taught us how to tat (make lace). I still have the shuttle, but I no longer can remember how to tat. Sewing seemed to come naturally. My mother made a lot of our dresses and playwear. She had a portable Singer Sewing Machine in a wooden carrying case. We used to sit inside the inverted cover and pretend that it was a boat. Mother never met a machine that worked fast enough for her. During the war she replaced her Singer with a White treadle machine and I began to test my skills. Sewing is mostly a matter of being able to follow directions. I began serious sewing by making myself a maternity smock. I made shirts, shorts, and dresses. I made all of Mimi Sanchez's bridesmaid dresses. One Christmas I made a shirt for each man in the family and for each of my brothers.

Did you ever have a special hideaway or playhouse? What made it special?

Not that I remember. In the summer Mother would spread blankets over the clothes lines and make us a tent to protect us from the sun. The only escape from the heat and humidity was in the cellar where we rode our tricycles and played ball and board games. As for a hideaway, I never relished having a separate secret place for myself or myself and my friends. There was always a strong desire in me to know Reality and plumb the depths of life. I was captivated by this desire from early on and I resented any attempts by others to sugar coat things or to protect me from the life I felt that I had been born to live to the fullest. I was an odd child probably, but I was wholly preoccupied in observing others and their behavior and in examining circumstances and relationships. When we lived near the woods, I was still in the primary grades. I loved to wander under the trees and I had a favorite place where I would sit and think. When I was twelve, we also lived on a beautiful wood where I went to be alone and take in life. In Santa Cruz, I would climb to the top of Laurentian Hill and lie on my back in the tall grass and watch the skies and <u>think</u> about life.

Did you ever go camping with your family? Where? Record one exceptional camping experience?

I first went camping as a Girl Scout when I was 14 years old. We had an outstanding leader named Carolyn Leonard who was a social worker. Gas was rationed, but Carolyn collected stamps from everyone so that she could transport the troop to Big Basin in the Santa Cruz Mountains to camp for a week. We slept in sleeping bags on the ground under the stars and cooked our own meals often sharing them with the deer that wandered through our campsite. We hiked and swam and played games. At night there was a campfire. We were about fifteen girls ages 13 to 15 and good friends. The most memorable camping experience was the six day stay at Idyllwild with Mom, Tom, Ruth, Michael, Judy, Doris and two month old Lisa. It was the week after Labor Day and the weather had taken a turn from warm and sunny to chilly and windy. Mom and I moved the two tents from the wind, boiled diapers and draped them everywhere to dry, took cat baths in buckets of water and layered all of our clothes. It was an adventure for us but even more so for the kids.

Who gave you your name and why? Did you have a family nickname? How did get it?

I was named Gladys after Gladys Hoffman, a friend of my parents. My mother sometime jokingly called me "Happy Bottom". It was in high school that I was first tagged "Red". I liked it and it stuck. Even the parents of my friends called me Red and I'm certain that some of them didn't know my proper name. I remember visiting the mother of my dear friend, Betty Cain Criss, when she was in her mid 90's. I knocked at the door and called in. Then I said, "It's someone out of your past." She responded, "I know who you are. How are you Red?". Even when I meet old classmates its, "Hi Red". I have a strong attachment to my name, despite the fact that I would never have chosen it. Try as I might, I can never think of one more fitting and to change it would cause a real identity crisis. After all Gladys is the name my parents called me and my grandparents and all of the significant and casual persons with whom I came in contact. I am Gladys Marie Curran Kehr. All of my transactions that require a signature are proudly signed Gladys M. Kehr. Gladys is a Celtic name (in France it is Claude). The name means "lame". Tacho even found a St. Gladys who was a Queen of England early on in the third century, I think.

Who was you favorite teacher? Why?

Mary Louise Krug, I.H.M. was a little woman who was born in Muncie, IN. Her mother was of Irish descent and her father was of German heritage. The family came to Los Angeles when Mary Louise was eight years old. Her father was an accountant and he and Mary Louise had a close loving relationship. When the class of '48 descended on St. Anthony, we were the usual freshmen prepared by eight years of the discipline imposed on Catholic school students for more of the same. From the first Mary Louise related to us as persons worthy of her respect. Of course, that impressed us. Without exception we loved her and strived to be equal to her expectations. She was a history scholar who was intent on teaching us much more than the record of past events. Through her grasp of world history she was able to show us how the most seemingly insignificant decisions precipitated war and had an impact on future developments in society. Late in her life, she spent a weekend with me at Ryden's house in San Clemente. As we drove around Orange County she amazed me with her knowledge of the persons and families and transactions that had formed our county just as she had on so many occasions shown me Los Angeles, California, the Church and the world.

Who was the first person to talk to you about God? What effect did this have on you?

My Daddy spoke to me of God from the days when I was a very young child. He was so consistent in his attitude that everything I was and had was due to God's loving care that I have never doubted it. My Mother was also intent on leading us to God. She often proposed that I might pray for health, for God's blessing, for His forgiveness. When I began school, my formal knowledge of God increased due to the teaching of the Sisters and Priests who gave us instructions. Sr. Felicity, one of my first grade teachers, reinforced God's love for me. In the fifth grade, Sr. Incarnate, a very young Sister from Connecticut on the mainland, shared with me her faith in God's love and encouraged me to respond to Him always. Sr. Beatrice, my seventh grade teacher, caused me to see that I don't live in a vacuum and that everything I say and do has consequences. If I had thought beyond myself before this time, I might have realized the implications of this proposal. I know that her teaching came to me like a divine revelation that changed my life because I saw, as if for the first time, that I had been empowered by God to be a force for good and that I had been given an awesome responsibility.

Where did you go to grade school? Junior High? High School? Tell me about your best childhood friend.

St. Rose of Lima, Haddon Heights, NJ, Bender Academy, Elizabeth, NJ, Holy Name School, Camden, NJ, St. John, Collingswood, NJ, Blessed Sacrament, Elizabeth, NJ, St. Vincent, Newport News, VA, St. Cecilia, Pennsauken, NJ, Our Lady of Good Counsel, Moorestown, NJ, St. Augustine, Honolulu, T.H. (Waikiki), St. Anthony, Honolulu. T.H. (Kalihi Kai), St. Ann, Wildwood, NJ, Sacred Heart, Hyattsville, Md., Holy Cross, Santa Cruz, CA. I heartily disliked St. Rose of Lima, St. Cecilia and Sacred Heart Schools. My favorite was Holy Cross in Santa Cruz. Mary Ellen Conrado was my best friend there. Then there was St. Anthony in Long Beach where I went for four years to high school. There are few experiences which I value so highly. There are irreplaceable memories of teachers, friends and associates that gave me a sense of belonging, a place in society for which I am deeply grateful. Betty Cain was my best friend. In fact, I felt like a member of her family as well as my own. I would often walk home with her and then continue on my walk, a few miles, to my own house. We shared everything and I still esteem her friendship and feel a deep affection for her. She was one of the beautiful people in my life.

What was the most tender day in your childhood?

The night before we were evacuated from Honolulu, Claire and Raymond LeBer went with us to P.Y. Chong's Teahouse on the Ala Moana canal. Daddy and Raymond traded quips with P.Y. #1 China cook and made light conversation and romantic remarks to their respective wives. I remember the climate of this occasion and the lanterns swinging from the ceiling. I knew that we were going home to the mainland, the full import of out situation hadn't hit home. Raymond and Claire drove us to the pier where the S.S. Aquitania was tied up. It was a huge ship with four smoke stacks. Daddy hugged all of us and kissed us goodbye. We went, Mother, Pat, Jane, Larry and Jimmy and myself up the gangplank and through the baffles erected to maintain the blackout aboard ship. We were taken to a stateroom once beautiful but now stripped down for wartime use that contained three sets of bunks. Mother sat down on the edge of the lower bunk. She was holding Jimmy in her arms and there were tears in her eyes. She said to me, "Gladys, you will have to help me now because Daddy won't be with us". Only those who know the depth of my Mother's independence can understand how pressured by the crises of the preceding months she must have felt. And I felt privileged in her having shared her need with me. In the morning, Easter Sunday, April 5, 1942, we sailed.

What mischievous childhood experience do you remember?
How did it affect you?

When we lived in Newport News, VA. there was a census. It must have been a local or a state census because it was 1938 and the U.S. census is taken every ten years e.g. 1940. When a man knocked on our door I went with my Mother to see who it was. After a short explanation the man began to ask my Mother questions, her name and age and my Dad's name, age and occupation. My Mother was as usual compliant. When the census taker proceeded to ask the name, ages and relationship of the other members of the household I protested. "Don't tell him my name. It's none of his business". Of course Mother reprimanded me and sent me to my room, but as well as I knew that I had at the least a stern "talking to" in the offing, I felt betrayed by my own Mother. I bristled at the fact that Mother had allowed an outsider to invade my privacy. Any punishment for my "misbehavior" was negligent compared to how this incident affected me. To this day I will respond to lawful inquiries by those who are authorized to ask. I will not give myself away piece by piece for capricious reasons.

What was your favorite meal when you were a child?
What made it your favorite?

Roast beef and mashed potatoes and gravy with corn for a vegetable. I liked to layer all of these on top of my potatoes and add little pieces of bread and pepper and salt. That was the best, but if my parents noticed I was advised to desist from such a concoction. My Mother made the best baked beans that I have ever tasted. She baked them in a large cast iron skillet and the sauce was thick and syrupy. I have never been able to make them that well. Mommom, my Mother's Mother, was a great cook. I especially remember her "Hot Slaw"—shredded cabbage fried in lard and seasoned with sugar and vinegar. I remember coming home from school to a huge stack of freshly made doughnuts. There was a salad dressing that my Mother made from her Mother's recipe, a combination of vinegar, evaporated milk, sugar and pepper and salt. Sticky buns were a specialty with Mom. Dough with raisins and cinnamon inside, dripping with brown sugar syrup and pecans are a welcome taste. And there was also Cottage Pudding—pound cake with a hot sauce made from water, cornstarch, sugar, butter and vanilla.

What summer games and activities did your family enjoy?

Summer was a magical time but only as the sun went down. It was hot and humid in the summer and on the East coast the heat did not cease at sundown. Most nights we slept only in panties with an electric fan on all night long. So the evening held no relief but the darkness and the games we played were a large distraction. First there were the fireflies. As soon as darkness fell the flickering lights had us in hot pursuit until we captured them and put them in large jars with air holes in the lid and pieces of grass and leaves inside for their sustenance. All of the children in the neighborhood would be outside and while parents sat on the front steps and watched or visited with each other we would play Hide and Seek, Red Rover or Here Comes the Dukes a Riding in the middle of the street and in our yards. The enchantment of being out in the dark sometimes to 9 PM or later was a real treat. There was sometimes ice cream too after our games were over. Then it was up the "wooden hill", as Poppop called the stairs, to bed. I disliked the summer because of the way that heat affected me. It was intolerable. I would lie down with a book in the hammock that hung in our oak tree or in the grass on the shady side of the house by the Lily of the Valley, but night did come!

What kind of prayer did you say before you went to sleep?
Who taught you how to pray it?

In the name of the Father, and of the Son, and of the Holy Ghost, Amen. Now I lay me down to sleep. I pray the Lord my soul to keep. If I should die before I wake, I pray the Lord my soul to take. God bless Mother and Daddy, Mommom and Poppop, my sisters and brothers, all my aunts and uncles and cousins and make me a good girl. Angel of God, my guardian dear, to whom God's love commits me here. Ever this day be at my side, to light, to guard, to rule and guide. Amen. In the name of the Father, and of the Son and of the Holy Ghost. Amen. Daddy taught me the Sign of the Cross and knelt with me beside my bed holding my hands flat upright with my thumbs forming a cross while we prayed. But before prayers, my mother would read me a chapter from a favorite book and a chapter of Bible History. I would have to say that Mother and Daddy religiously spent time with us in the evening talking and listening, telling stories and singing to us and obviously enjoying it. There was a WWI song, "Just Break the News to Mother" which would always bring Pat to tears. And Mom and Dad dancing the Grapevine and the Buck and Wing. It was a happy time for all of us.

What responsibilities did your parents require of you as a child? Explain how this affected your growth and development.

To set an example for the other children was my prime responsibility. As the oldest, I was expected to be in charge, to keep an eye out for the younger children. To think for myself and to dare to be different. From the time that I was quite small, I often heard my Daddy deliver this message. He was intent on my cherishing my own tradition and the revelations that I been given not only what he had shown me, but what I had learned from experience. My Dad always shared with me his life experience, his feelings at various times of crisis and the choices he had to face as well as his response to God that was his ultimate consideration. He knew that I took my responsibility to heart and he never failed to remind me when I might have gone off course. Our arguments or shouting matches stemmed from my being so much his child and reminding him when he didn't want to hear what he had taught me.

What childhood memory first comes to mind when you think about winter? How do you respond to that memory?

Sitting nervously in the classroom sneaking peeks at the first snowfall of the season and trying to act attentive when the only thought in my head was how soon the teacher would release us. When she did there was an undercurrent of excitement that carried us out the door where a manic dance took place. Spinning, diving, jumping to catch the elusive snowflakes which melted in our hands. But anticipation of a snow covered landscape remained despite our failure to catch hold of nature and create the scene for ourselves. I have at times awakened in the middle of the night and viewed the sleeping world from my window. On one December night when we lived in Greenbelt, Maryland, I woke to such stillness and beauty that I have never forgotten it. Snow blanketed the house down below and all the trees and shrubs. The ground was dazzling white even in the pale moonlight and the street lamps seemed only a quaint decoration. The scene outside of the window of our Pullman car as I lay in the lower berth on my first trip West was spectacular. We were crossing the Great Salt Lake as dawn broke over the snow covered mountains casting a rosy glow on the whole scene.

What toys did you like to play with? Why those particular toys?

Roller skates, balls, jacks, marbles and a jump rope. My first roller skates were made with a leather piece that fit over the toes and were the same as key skates. I can still remember seeing Daddy walking toward us on the way home from work with two boxes under his arm. The boxes contained Union Hardware roller skates and skate keys, a skate key on a piece of white twine around one's neck. We had "arrived", another surprise of my parents. We lived on roller skates. There were new games every week that involved a ball and many of them could be played alone. Jacks went along with us everywhere and they came out not only when someone said, "Let's play Jacks", but also when there was a lull in our activities. We liked marbles, shooters, aggies, alloys, steelies, glassies, cat's eye, immies, peewees, etc. I coveted all, but some more than others. I had quite a collection. Every kid also had a length of clothesline for a jump rope which went to school and came out at every recess. Long lines formed to jump and skip and touch the ground, turn around, jump hot pepper and double Dutch. I forgot pen knives for mumbly peg, a game where a knife was thrown into a circle in the dirt to lay claim to parts of the circle.

What were your youthful goals and ambitions for life? Which ones have you been able to fulfill?

I have met very few persons who had youthful goals that they could formulate. Some individuals can tell you that they want to be a doctor, a teacher, a lawyer, an engineer or a nurse but that seems to me a means rather than an end. For some persons the articulation of a goal has never been a necessity. For others the accomplishments of their work to completion was enough. The goal of one's life ultimately is to be one with Christ in responding to God's love. The labor or recognizing and accepting the positives and negatives in oneself, of remaining still and acknowledging God's power to birth once again is the only way to wholeness. In this process the Paschal Mystery of the birth, death and resurrection are enacted over and over. A desire to recreate "family" as I have known it was a driving force in my life. I believe that despite all the inconsistencies that appear, God Who gave me the desire will fulfill it. I pray always that God through all the crooked lines of our lives will teach us His love, make us through His Holy Spirit one with Christ and reunite us in eternal joy.

What did your family like to do on weekends? Describe one particularly memorable event.

We walked for miles and threw ourselves into nature. On the day before Jane was born we covered the whole town including the cemetery, the park and the surrounding countryside. There was a place called Bancroft School with an open field next to it where we would feed the sheep through the fence and pick buttercups. In the park grew huge oaks and chestnut trees. I remember Daddy pointing out to me these trees and reciting the poem about the village blacksmith. I liked to swing in the little wooden swings with the bar in front as Daddy pushed me up into the air and I fell back into his arms. This was one of my images of God as Father. Sunday was a very quiet day, no skating or playing ball or making noise of any kind. In the morning after Mass there was the Sunday paper with the colored funnies. Maggie and Jiggs, The Little King, Good Deed Dotty, Etta Kett, Orphan Annie, etc. Dinner was special, usually with a roast and all the fixings. Sunday evening was for the enjoyment of Edgar Bergen and Charlie McCarthy, Jack Benny and the Fitch Bandwagon on radio. And so to bed!

What scent or sound immediately takes you back to childhood? Describe the feeling it evokes.

Humus, the rich, dark soil of New Jersey and certain weeds and trees and flowers, lilac, lily of the valley, hyacinth, and tea roses. It is very humid in New Jersey and in the springtime the air is laden with the scent of flowers in bloom. Certain trees have such an odor that I am as a child again in the woods where the moss and white violets grow. Water, the odor of a swimming pool takes me back to Mountwell Park and swimming in only my panties. I loved the water, the only relief from the tortuous heat of summer which I could barely tolerate. I could smell ocean air long before I arrived at the seashore and I could luxuriate all day by the side of a bubbling brook Incense and beeswax candles, the silence and the pageantry of the liturgy moved me deeply. Lavender and lilacs and newly mown grass, mint leaves, carnation leis, camphor balls of Mother's cedar chest. The fresh clean odor of sheets hung to dry in the open air, the smell of onions and beef roasting and of doughnuts hot from the kettle, the Palmolive soap in Aunt Jettie's bathroom and Camay in ours, rubbing alcohol and Vick's Vapo Rub all evoke memories of home. Marching bands and Mother and Daddy whistling thrilled me. Gardenia corsages on Prom Night!

Were you baptized or dedicated as an infant? If so, where and by whom?

Due to the fact that my Dad and Mother had eloped to Media, Pa. to marry I was not baptized until they were married in the Church in December of 1931. My Godparents were my Uncle Bill, Daddy's brother, and Gladys Hoffman, a friend of my parents. Both my Dad and Mother were people of deep faith in God and they imparted their faith to me through my life. As a small child they taught me to pray, read me stories from the Bible and talked to me about ways that God intervenes in my life. They always made it a point to explain the moral choices involved in any given situation. I believe deeply that it was through my Baptism that Jesus saved me and made me His own. In times of suffering and trials the memory of God having chosen me then and at so many times in my life has sustained me and given me the courage to go on. I remember especially one of the times when I was very low in spirits. Kenny had quit paying child support, Memorarie Guild was up for sale; I was alone with three children, no means of support and feeling removed from God. I prayed the Apostle's Creed and that made all the difference.

Were you ever in a Christmas program? How did you respond to the experience?

In the 7th grade we had a Christmas program in which I was a character named Tinsel. I wore a white gown with streamers of tinsel hanging down the front and the back and the sleeves. I don't remember the plot of the play but my lines were as follows:

> My name is Tinsel
> A task is mine
> For jolly oh Santa I shine and shine
> From bough to bough of the
> Christmas tree
> I flash and dangle, its fun for me.

I think I was chosen because my voice carried. Some would have said I was a loud mouth. I found it exciting. Pat and I were in a Christmas program in the 6th grade (Pat 5th) also. It was the enactment of the Nativity story. We both knew all the parts and songs and we used to go through the whole play at night in bed. "Winds through the olive trees softly did blow round little Bethlehem long long ago, I was also Babushka (Russian Grandmother) in the 3rd grade for the school Christmas program.

When did you become a Christian? How did your life change?

My life began as a result of Sister Beatrice's teaching in that I became more reflective. I began to make associations between the teachings of the Church and the events of everyday life. I was preparing for Confirmation and there was a deeper meaning that evolved from my studies. About this time I experienced a sudden fear of damnation that I hadn't known before. This fear overtook me on several occasions for no apparent reason after the lights were out and I was about to go to sleep. I was fearful of never awakening, of going to hell. Now I realize that it was probably due to my taking a more determined acceptance of God's love because St. Ignatius cites the presence of evil to one committed to following Christ as the source of fear, confusion and other negative emotions. Then there was peace. We moved to San Diego shortly after this and three months later on to Long Beach. I enrolled at St. Anthony High School in the Fall of 1944. I was bereft as the loss of so many good friends and for a time feeling all alone. One day Sr. Mary Louise (Krug) made the announcements of committee heads for the Sodality. I was appointed head of the Eucharistic Committee. That committee put out the vestments and vessels for Mass and set the markers for the Scripture readings of the day.

Where was your childhood home located? Did you enjoy living there?

Which one? I was born in Pottstown, Pa. (York Street). Then we moved to Haddonfield, NJ where we lived on Fowler Avenue, King's Highway and Lee Avenue. Then we went to Coca Beach, Fla. for a few months after which we returned to Camden, NJ. We lived in two different apartments on 4th Street and the second on 6th Street before we moved to a house on Kresson Road in Haddonfield, NJ. Mommom and Poppop lived on Colonial Avenue and when I was 5 years old we went to live with them. After that there were the houses on McPhelan Avenue and Atlantic Avenue from which we went to Burnham Road in Elizabeth, NJ. When Dad's job finished we returned to Camden, NJ to a house on 6th Street and to Bailey Street. Our next residence was in Collingswood, NJ on Summerfield Avenue before we headed north again to Elizabeth where we lived in an upstairs flat on Madison Avenue. I was in 3rd grade when we went to Newport News, Va. and lived on Blair Avenue. The next stop was 41st Street in Pennsauken, NJ then on to Stanwyck Road and 3rd Street in Moorestown, NJ. In Honolulu, T.H. we lived in Waikiki on Ena Road and on Kaliki and in Pearl Harbor on Plantation Road. Home again we lived on 12th Street in Wildwood, NJ on Ridge Route in Greenbelt, MD. In Santa Cruz, Ca. we made our home on Bay Street, Main Street and Anthony and then it was off to San Diego, Ca. and Mc Candless Avenue.

What chores did you have to do when you were growing up? Did you get an allowance? How much was it?

We didn't have many set chores (setting the table and clearing it and washing and drying the dishes), but we were taught to take responsibility for ourselves and our home. I was taught to make my bed, to clean a bathroom, to cook, etc., however, my major chore was to take care of my things to hang up my clothes or put them away or in the laundry, to clean up after myself in any area of the house that I used. These rules were learned early and enforced consistently. I was the oldest of eight children and we lived in a comfortable and orderly home. None of us would have even thought of disrupting this order and walking away leaving a mess. Not only my Mother's, but also my Dad's view forced this lifestyle by expecting of us consideration of the comfort, time and energy of those who shared our home. Babysitting was left to Mommom on the rare occasions when we did not accompany my parents. Of course, when I was twelve or so I was given more responsibility for the care of the younger children, but this was usually in the daytime. We didn't receive an allowance for doing our duty, but we were given money for the show or a soda or magazine.

What was the name of your favorite pet? Why was it your favorite?

Blackie our dog, which my Daddy had rescued from a spiked fence on which she was impaled, was a very docile pet. We trussed her like a baby dressing her in castoff baby clothes, putting her in Poppop's Morris chair, carefully and lovingly tucking her in and then our chore completed retiring to play some other game. As soon as our attention left her, she would jump out of the chair and try to shed her baby costume. When we lived on Madison Avenue in Elizabeth, NJ my Dad brought home from the bar on Christmas Eve a nervous puppy who spent the next two weeks running about with the "runs" until Mother was worn out cleaning up after it. Exit puppy. On Constitution Lane Larry encouraged a beautiful Irish Setter to follow him home from school and he was determined to keep it. Daddy let it go and the next day to compensate Larry for his loss, he brought home a tiny brown and white puppy. Skippy grew to be a huge hound. When Daddy came home, he would jump up and stand on his hind legs with his paws on Daddy's shoulders and yap as if he was talking to him. Tommy, Ruth and Michael could do anything to Skippy and he never turned on them. Once when Skippy returned from one of his conquests bruised and weary, they wrapped him in a blanket, applied a heating pad and read him stories.

If you learned to play a musical instrument, tell me your memories of lessons, practice, and your music teacher. If not, what instrument did you want to play and why?

When I was in the second grade, I was able to persuade my parents to allow me to take music lessons. I don't remember how I ended up with the violin which in the hands of a neophyte is hardly melodious. This was probably the reason that I lost interest almost immediately in that instrument. I forced myself to practice for a month or two. Then to the relief of myself and the whole family I returned the violin.

I always loved the piano. When I was a sophomore in high school or maybe a junior or senior, I was earning enough money to afford lessons. Since we didn't own a piano I practiced on a piano at school. I had high hopes. I learned to play with my right hand and with my left hand separately. I never could coordinate both hands. Since then I have left music to the more talented. If I had had any musical talent I would have preferred the piano. I also love the harp and the cello. Great composers, Mozart and Sibelius.

Describe one of your favorite dress-up outfits as a child. On what occasions would you wear it?

Dress up outfits? When I was young every little girl had a stack of hats, jewelry, suits (men's and woman's), dresses, coats and shoes, which whether it was extensive or limited, provided many hours of enjoyment. These castoffs were donated by parents, grandparents, aunts and uncles and were used to act out our interpretation of the adults in our lives. We definitely had favorite costumes. I have always loved clothes and see in them one way of expressing who I am. As for dress-up outfits in the sense of clothes that I wore in our normal round of activities—a lovely green (pale) crotched dress with a wide collar that Mother made that I ruined on first wearing by spilling grape juice on it at the Church carnival, a gold, green and plaid cotton dress with a white pointed collar made by Mother, a red dress with an umbrella skirt and puffed sleeves, two sun suits (red, white and blue and rose colored), a navy and white tweed Sears princess style coat and a navy tam, a long waisted style coat dress, a lavender voile dress that Mom made for my confirmation and a gold sundress that Mom made for me when I was fourteen and a coat that Mom made for me when I was ten with a dyed rabbit fur collar that puffed up to my ears.

Describe your childhood bedroom. What was the view from your window?

Which one? Going to bed was at the bottom of my list of priorities. I spent little time in my room unless I was punished and sent there to contemplate an infraction of the rules. And further in a very secure childhood, the place in which we lived was ever changing. My parents room, I remember well—The beautiful golden yellow and turquoise bedroom suite which was Mom's and Dad's wedding present, the white spread embroidered with a basket of flowers, my mother's mother of pearl manicure set and the china lamps. Only sitting in a chair in my bedroom when I was punished for opening the cellar door and Larry tumbled down the steps, but then there was bed, which I shared with Pat. A front bedroom upstairs where I had chickenpox, a rear bedroom upstairs where I came down with scarlet fever, a large bedroom over the front porch with dormer windows out onto the roof and the darkened bedroom where I had the measles come to mind. There was a room at the top of the stairs where I listened to my parents talking and to the radio reports of the Spanish Civil War and was terrified and another where I was able to read Robin Hood by the hall light. Most memorable was a large upstairs room wallpapered in tiny yellow roses and trees outside the window in Moorestown, NJ.

Describe what the family room looked like when you were a child.

We had a Morris chair which was a fore-runner of the recliner. It had an iron bar across the back which could be moved to adjust the slant of the chair back. It belonged to my grandfather, but it was used as a bed when we where sick. Sometimes we would put our dog Blackie there dressed in clothes and pretend that she was our baby. We had an oval wicker table that was dark brown which we could drape with a blanket to make a tent. It had a lamp on it. There was also a wicker couch (or settee). The table had a crocheted doily. There was also a non-burning fireplace. Pictures were the only decoration in the somewhat austere setting. The Victorian age had passed and with it had gone the fussy frilly bric-a-brac of former years. The dining room opened out from the living room. There was a round oak pedestal table and a massive buffet and wooden side chairs with replacable composition seats. Pat once lost her ball and put her head under the buffet looking for it and her head became stuck. I remember sitting at the table while the grown-ups drank their coffee and talked over the news of the day.

*Describe a frightening or difficult experience from childhood.
How did you respond to it?*

We were up before 8:00 AM to eat breakfast and to dress to attend Sunday Mass at Pearl Harbor Naval Base a short distance away. Within the hour the sky was full of planes with the Rising Sun of Japan on the wings. We assumed that they were involved in war game maneuvers, but it was unusual to see this in a populated area. The Army Base was across the street from our house and from our house we had often witnessed the take offs and landings at this base called Hickam Field. By the time we left for Church the whole neighborhood was buzzing with comments about this unusual sight. We were within sight of the gate to the Navy Yard when a Navy Chief came running toward us yelling for us to take cover that this was war. Daddy took us home and left for the base where he helped man fire hoses trained on the burning ships. At home we put six week old Jimmy in a dresser drawer in the corner of the living room. I remember vividly being at my bedroom window when a plane with a Japanese airman standing at a machine gun in the side of the plane came within twenty feet of our house. I prayed spontaneously for the first time and continued throughout the day.

Describe your grandparents' house. Did you visit them often? Why or why not?

When I was a toddler, the home of my grandparents was my home also. It was a comfortable home which showed the care and the industry and the creativity of my grandparents. It was a place of security and warmth and love. Poppop was all mine probably, because Pat was very timid, so I shadowed him when he went to the cellar to his huge wooden tool box with his name carved on it in beautiful script or polished the mallet with the wide brass bands or repaired the rungs of chair. In that cellar hung Poppop's tricycle with the large front wheel and the high seat. I loved being with Poppop also when he puttered in the garden. Mommom was larger than life inspiring one with the sense that everything was under control. I never remember her at rest. From the time that she pulled on her chemise until she slept (which I never saw) she was busy, mostly at the stove turning out awesome meals or over a pot of boiling starch or scrubbing clothes or running them through the wringer. She and my Mother manned flat irons every Tuesday and spent most of the day filling the lines across our kitchen with the beautifully ironed clothes. She made beds swiftly and efficiently pounding the devil out of the bolster. She could crochet without even seeming to notice. Rocking the baby took on a new dimension for the baby in her arms. She loved us mightily.

Describe a memorable Valentine you received.

Well, I cannot recall any Valentine that was particularly impressive, but I have received many letters and cards expressing the sender's love and regard for me that touched my heart. Letters from Mommom were few, but she always addressed me as someone beloved who she could count on. Florence Candia and Mickey Atkins from 5th and 6th grade demonstrated their affection in corresponding with me faithfully after we were separated. Aunts, uncles, cousins never forgot to send me greetings. When our Girl Scout leader enlisted in the Waves during WWII she continued to express her regard in writing to me regularly. Pat Ross, a pen pal from Santa Rosa, shared her life and her hopes with me for several years. After graduation Louis Dauw, a sailor I dated for a time, was a devoted correspondent. Kenny wrote frequently from San Diego and Korea. Then there was Isobel and an ongoing relationship and letters starting in 1957 until the present day. My brother, Jim, shared his life with me over the course of several years and showed me by his concern and constancy many confirmations of his love for me. I am always touched when some one takes the time to write to me. John Pierre and the other M.C. brothers were always intent on expressing their care, their confidence in me and their love.

Who gave you your first Bible and how old were you when you received it? How did it influence your life?

No one ever gave me a Bible. As a child I had a Bible History published by Benzinger Brothers in New York City. Every night my Mother would read me a story from the Old Testament. I have always remembered the story of Abraham who was asked to sacrifice his son Isaac and of Moses who persevered in prayer with his arms upraised to Yahweh until the Israelites were victorious. My Mother who learned scripture through years of Sunday School and Bible Study was given to using Proverbs to explain the mysteries of life. Of course, my most lasting impressions of the Holy Spirit in the Word of God came from meditation on the Scripture read at Mass or in reading the Bible in private. In school also we were taught the basis of our belief in God our Creator, His providential care for His people, the Covenant God made and His promise to send us a Savior as well as the birth, life and death and resurrection of Jesus and the traditions that were established as a result of His teaching. I have also taken in many hours of Bible Study, but I found in reading the Word prayerfully far greater fruit than my studies provided.

What was your favorite pastime as a child? Did you prefer doing it alone or with someone else?

Watching the grownups and listening to their conversations and their stories and going off on my own exploring. I was a people watcher and I still enjoy this pastime. Early on my Mother and Daddy played with Pat and me, sang to us, told us stories and read to us and took us for long walks. My Mother was intent on my posture and behavior on our walks. My Daddy would tell us about the people we passed, the trees, the bit of history and poetry various scenes inspired. My mother imparted more practical knowledge from time to time. They always showed us a good sense of humor, love and compassion for others and a tender care for us. My grandfather was disabled, but he planted our garden with vegetables and fixed anything that was broken. Sometimes he built beautiful wooden things like a tabernacle for Christ the King Church. He built a bench for Pat and me to sit on at the table. Mommom was a great cook, a bustling and volatile woman and a delight to observe. I liked my tricycle, balls, digging in the dirt, books and playing dress up. But the greatest fun was following where my curiosity led me and learning the "why" and "what fors" of life.

Tell about some Christmas rituals in your family and how you felt about them.

Christmas Eve was the one time of the year when the whole family within traveling distance of home came together. When I was little, we were put to bed early in a warm cozy bed in a house where there was no evidence of the impending activities. It was the custom that the adults put up the tree and decorated it on Christmas Eve while we slept. So the first time we saw the tree was Christmas morning. (One Christmas, Mother had put our gifts on lay away and Daddy went in Christmas Eve to buy a tree and pick them up. He did pick up gifts and stopped with them to refresh himself. He came home empty handed and had to be sent to search for the gifts and the tree. It was difficult to be angry at my Dad. He was the first to admit his wrong doing.) When we came to California it was the custom to prepare for the celebration weeks ahead of time and gradually we gave in. On Christmas Eve we all gathered around Mother and Daddy, the center of our lives. As we grew older and married and had children of our own this was Christmas. For me, Christmas was our being together. I dearly loved giving gifts especially to the children. I hoped that the gift exchange would help to keep alive the relationship between cousins and aunts and uncles who may be separated by distance.

What crazy fads do you remember in grade school?

As a pupil in Catholic school in the 1930's and early 1940's my life was circumscribed by the austerities of that era and the precepts that respectable people followed. Added to rules of behavior imposed by our culture, there was the maze of regulations, varying from school to school, that we obeyed vigorously to set an example to others, to maintain order and discipline and as a sign of courtesy. We wore uniforms to school so a dress code was already established. Whatever kind of shoes one had were accepted (lucky in those days to have shoes) and one's hairdo or haircut was the province of one's parents. There was no gum chewing or snacking in class, no speaking without being recognized by the teacher, no leaving one's seat without permission. In a sense we were perfect little automatons. If such adherence to rules taught one anything it was that my spirit was indomitable. I still had autonomy. My will was free. This realization has served me well throughout my life. When I have felt oppressed almost to the point of extinction, I have always kept in mind the two gifts that God demonstrated in giving me life—His love and free will.

What were some of the most memorable books you read as a child? What made them memorable?

Little Women and all the rest of Louisa May Alcott's books were favorites of mine probably because I was interested in history and how individuals coped in the face of changes in their lives. The Secret Garden was one of the children's books that appealed to me even though I read all of the classics. A book that Pat and I read (or rather a series) was about Elsie Dinsmore, a little Episcopal girl who seemed too prissy and pious to be real. I came to prefer stories about real people and autobiographies than biographies. I loved to read and there were always books in our house because our parents were also readers. Even though I had favorite books and enjoyed some types of a literature over others, I didn't discriminate if I was without a book to read. I read Charlie Chan, Earle Stanley Gardner, Faith Baldwin novels when I was about twelve. Then Owen Francis Dudley series about the Masterful Monk dealt with spiritual matters and they had a profound effect on me. I had read all of Mark Twain by the time I was ten years old. I remember agonizing over the loss of faith experiences by a young man who was paralyzed as the result of a skiing accident. About this time C.S. Lewis' The Screwtape Letters, the dialogue between the devil who was Screwtape and one of his workers describing the ways that a human being can be tricked and deceived into following a life of evil.

Share a story about a severe winter storm.

Actually two such storms come to mind. In March of 1952 or 1953 we traveled East by car to Springfield, MA. As we left Indianapolis it started snowing. By the time we got on the Pennsylvania Turnpike the snow was heavy and there were strong winds pummeling our little Austin. Kenny talked of stopping, but as we passed all the parked cars at the Howard Johnsons he would change his mind. By the time we got off the turnpike Kenny's legs were cramped from holding down the gas pedal all night. The Austin was a <u>little</u> sedan (4 cylinders, 4 speeds with the gear shift on the floor). When we lived on San Alto Way we had such heavy rains that the street flooded and there was water up to our top step. The worst storm was the one we went through on the way home from Mom's and Dad's in Bremerton, WA. in December 1964. It was already snowing in Portland, OR. in the afternoon and by the time we crossed over into CA. it was fierce. Snow was swirling against the windshield cutting visibility to almost zero. This went on for hours in a region without lights. When we had seen no other vehicles for hours we began to fear that we were lost, but we had no other choice but to go on. About 4 AM we reached the bustling little town of Weed, CA. where we had the most vile coffee I had ever tasted. We had been traveling over the Siskiyous on a closed highway.

If you went to college or to a career training school, where did you go and why?

When Kenny and I lived in our first home, my friend Isobel came up with the idea of taking a college course at night. We went to Long Beach City College and we took Psychology 1A from a very handsome Mr. Nelson. I actually went along for the ride in that I no desire to attend college. I had always enjoyed learning but I did not believe that a college education would take me where I wanted to go. No profession held any attraction and a career was the furthest thing from my mind. I found the experience interesting but a second best substitute to the real stuff of life. I have always found in the elitism that is fostered by the emphasis on formal education an ignorance of the knowledge that can be gained by living life fully and not only the knowledge, but more importantly the wisdom. Admittedly, teachers are influenced by central tendency (greatest good for the greatest number), but there is little recognition of other alternatives except in advanced studies. Suffice it to say that college education is a necessity for technical and scientific pursuits. But to emphasize the importance of acquiring knowledge intellectually is to devalue the wisdom that is beyond reason (but never opposed to reason) that can only come to one by the grace of God.

Where did you live when you were going to college or developing a career? Describe an unforgettable experience from that time in your life?

When I finally attended college my life was a shambles. Kenny's lifestyle offered no sense of security and there was an increasing sense of needing to provide for myself and the children. I was interested in Pastoral Counseling and aspects of healthcare that were just opening to the lay person. I had acquired some of the necessary experience to be accepted in the training program at St. Joseph Hospital. I was working for a large marketing company and I was in great demand for executive interviews. I could get into any office and I had good communication skills. In any event more education wouldn't hurt. Thanks to the disciplines of a Catholic education, I was miles ahead of my classmates. Thanks to my life experience, I wasn't taken in by my learned instructors whose teaching was sometimes limited by their reliance on books and the views of academia. I did not disdain research or the opinions of others or lack respect for those who taught me, but in me they did not find a tabula rosa. There were some few professors who took advantage of the captive audience to promulgate falsehood (laws of the Church which I knew well) or to promote a lopsided view of life.

As a teenager, did you belong to a club or church youth group? Tell me about the individuals in the group who were most significant to you.

The Anthonians was a club for young singles that I joined after I had graduated from high school. We had members from all over the country that had arrived here to work and had left all of their friends back home. It was a great place to make social contacts. The club was sponsored by St. Anthony Church and the membership was Catholic. We met every Tuesday night to take up the business and to dance. A bowling league was one of the popular weekly activities and in the summer there was the baseball team's schedule that was promoted with great enthusiasm. A yearly musical revue, trips to the mountains, beach parties, skating parties, hayrides, square dancing left little to be desired for entertainment. Don Bedard, who was a teacher, was our best man and later Dean of Cypress College where I studied in the '70's, Eddie Malone who I dated for a time was a fellow parishioner at St. Pius V and St. Justin. Barney Sullivan and Lee Susanka, Mary Redding and Al Susanka and Bob Wilcox all lived close by in St. Columban parish years later. The Hamilton brothers took our wedding pictures.

How did you learn to drive? What was your first car like?

A neighbor of ours, Ramon Soto, taught me to drive when I was seventeen. We did not have a car and the Sotos did. Off we would go down 20th Street to Santa Fe, through the industrial area on Anaheim Boulevard and right on Pico to the area around the canneries that bordered the L.A. River. One night unaware that I was heading straight for the river, necessity taught me how to make a sharp left turn. This was in a Ford with a stick shift on the floor. Driving in a city where buses where frequent was not a priority. When Kenny and I married we purchased a 1937 Plymouth for $110.00. We parked it at the curb at the folk's home when Kenny went overseas to Korea. I would drive it several times a week to keep the battery charged. In 1952 I took a few lessons and obtained my first license driving a 4 cylinder 1952 Austin with 4 speeds on the floor. My first car was a huge gray Hudson shaped like an inverted bathtub for which we paid $100.00. I drove Judy, Doris, Tommy, Ruthie, Michael and schoolmates to St. Pius V for school with Lisa in tow. Since then I have driven a wide variety of vehicles under many different circumstances and I've always enjoyed the experience.

What fashions were popular when you were in high school? Did you like them? Why or why not?

Sloppy Jocs. That is men's shirts and oversized sweaters with jeans rolled up to the knees. My Dad ruled that I could wear such a getup for beach parties, horseback riding, etc., but I couldn't wear jeans on the bus. I would take them with me and change clothes for the occasion. Sweaters or blouses and skirts were the usual garb for school with saddle shoes or penny loafers and bobby sox. Bandanas were popular worn over one's hair and tied under the chin or like a turban with all one's hair (in pin curls or loose piled underneath.) We weren't allowed to wear them like turbans to school. I had a tan and white hound's-tooth suit that I loved. I bought myself a cocoa colored coat at Buffum's for $40.00 when I was a senior that was very becoming. Blouses buttoned down the back with rows of tucks and pleats down the front and straight skirts with a slit from mid-calf to the knees and pleated plaids were my favorites. An expensive crepe blouse for dress sold for $7.00. For $75.00 I could buy 3 good quality skirts at Desmond's and 3 comparable sweaters at Buffum's. And—the hats—I always liked nice clothes and dressing up.

When did you have your first date? Tell me about it.

I was about sixteen years old when the son of one of the families who we knew from Church asked me to go out with his buddy. Russell was out of school about a year. He had joined the Navy and he was stationed at San Diego. His buddy, Ivar Kipp, was from Caldwell, Idaho. He was very attractive and he had a good sense of humor and a nice smile. We dated several times bowling, going to the movies and to The Pike (The Pike was a boardwalk and amusement park at the foot of Pine Avenue). Simultaneously I dated Eddie Larwood who was a quiet, shy fellow about four years older than I. We didn't date often. In fact my Dad used to say, "I've been meaning to call you, Gladys, but there was the Civil War, the Spanish American War, etc." Eddie was not the type who I would have sought but he was a very nice person. I could always count on him taking me to the Boat Races on Alamitos Bay on Memorial Day and to see the Harlem Globetrotters and he took me to a formal dance in Pasadena once a year and elsewhere when the mood moved him.

How far did you have to travel to attend elementary school, junior high and high school, and how did you travel to get there?

In the first grade my school was in another town so I took a school bus at the corner of our street. The next year, even though I went to two different schools, I walked. I remember the brick sidewalks, the smell of saloons as they swept them out, walking in the rain with a raincoat that hit the top of my galoshes, my book bag and the friends that joined one on the way. In winter there were snow suits and gloves to keep me warm. In second grade Pat and I walked together. We had a longer walk to St. Cecilia's. When we lived in Virginia we took the city bus to school.

One day my Mother met us and rode home on the bus too. I had a collection of marbles which I kept in my pencil box. I dropped the pencil box and marbles rolled around the bus all the way home and I really heard about that from Mother and Daddy. In Hawaii, Larry started school and I felt very grown up in being held responsible for him. In Wildwood at St. Ann we walked about fifteen blocks picking up about six friends along the way, but in Maryland we had to ride a bus to school again. I was happiest at Holy Cross where we walked all the way across town. I just noticed that we traveled by bus to all the schools I didn't like.

Did you ever travel abroad? How old were you and where did you go? Did you travel alone or with a group?

Dad accepted a job at Pearl Harbor Navy Yard and left for Honolulu, T.H. in September 1940. We were living on 3rd Street in Moorestown, NJ. We had an early winter with snow before Halloween. Mom had just sent the winter coats to the cleaners when she received orders for us to embark for Hawaii also. Besides retrieving the coats there was a mad rush to find appropriate clothes, pack and entrain four days later (December 10, 1940) from Philadelphia. In those days train travel was luxurious. We had, my Mom and four children, the entire Pullman car to ourselves except for Emily Hunt, a young New York society deb who was being sent to California to forget an undesirable boyfriend. She was full of fun. We arrived in San Francisco, California in the middle of a thunder storm and stayed at the Presidio before embarking on the Republic. We went through the Golden Gate, passing under the Golden Gate Bridge, past the flying fish to the open sea. On the first night out a storm sent waves breaking over the bow of the ship and down the passageway but except for some rough seas, a peaceful voyage. On Christmas Eve near midnight we reached port at Oahu to fireworks, a band playing Aloha Oe and flower leis. But most especially there was Daddy!

What extracurricular activities were you involved in during high school? Why did you choose those activities?

G.A.A. "Girls Athletic Association". I was not an athlete but I enjoyed my relationship with several girls who were Doc, Ruth Anne, Elva. And the games in which they played awoke in me the only competitive spirit that I ever experienced. I am impatient with games, just wanting them to be over except when our school was involved. I was on the B team as the timekeeper. Sodality of Our Lady. Mary Louise appointed me an officer as a new and utterly unknown freshman. We promoted participation in the Mass, in missionary work and a deepening intimacy with Christ. The Paduan (school newspaper) and the yearbook (Anthonian) staff reporting, taking pictures, doing layouts, etc. I was librarian which kept me abreast of what was good literature and what was new. I was for all four years a member of the Glee Club singing Alto in liturgical celebrations, shows, radio spots and at the Navy Hospital during WWII. I was responsible for keeping the popcorn machine filled and I was in great demand for eating leftovers from people's lunches.

Tell me about your first job.

My first job was at Dominican Hospital in Santa Cruz where I delivered meals to patients and fed them if they were unable to feed themselves. That was 1944. In the summer of 1945 Pat and I decided to attend summer school. We took typing which from the first left me cold. There was also a course being offered training girls as Nurses Aides. During World War II there was a great shortage of nurses because many of them were in the service. At the end of the course we were given the opportunity of working 20 hours a week at Seaside Memorial Hospital. We were paid 50 cents an hour, a great sum in those days; I began work on 2A a medical floor. Then I worked on 3E taking care of little children. From there I went to 4A where the elite medical and surgical patients were confined. I left there to work on 3D for Miss Betty Brogan, a saucy, proper little Irisher from McKeesport, PA. By the time I started on 3D I had passed the age of 16; I could be employed for 40 hours a week. This was an insurance floor (medical insurance was uncommon) and we had medical and surgical patients with all manner of ailments. When I graduated I had a steady job waiting for me that paid $150.00 a month. An R.N. received $180.00 a month. I quit when I was carrying Doris.

Describe your first trip alone.

After my freshman year of high school, a friend of mine, Virginia Anfang, invited me to accompany her on a three weeks vacation to a home her parents had in Round Valley outside Bishop, CA. We left by Greyhound about 7 PM on a June evening and traveled up 395 through the desert. It was my first experience of the suffocating desert that in summer is debilitating at night as it is in daytime. In the wee hours of the morning we made a rest stop at Lone Pine and the heavenly air-conditioned truck stop where I consumed half a cantaloupe. I have always remembered that snack, as I eat cantaloupe as a real lifesaver. By the time we hit Bishop, I had little hope that I would survive. We proceeded to Round Valley in the family station wagon. There was a little house on about three acres. It had a small pond fed by runoff from the mountains and the water was icy cold. I spent a lot of time sitting in that pond. Ginny and I slept out under the stars in a double bed on a side porch. We would see the lights of autos snaking their way up Sherman Pass into Nevada. There were chickens on the ranch and I killed and plucked a couple of chickens while I was there. One day we drove to Mono Lake and on another we took a picnic to a place called the Gorge, a deep ravine on the side of a mountain, and the first coolness in the whole trip. I only lasted two of the three weeks.

Tell me about a time when God answered a specific prayer for you.

In 1972, my life was rapidly falling apart. On the advice of our counselor I had given to Kenny the management of our finances. Further, I was to get a job, keep my wages and the amount I earned to myself. These suggestions were based on the fact that Kenny was erratic about paying the bills (I was in one day faced with the shut off of the electric and the water and large deposits to have service restored and the bank balance was $600.00). It was a constant hassle to obtain food money and I was given $10.00 a day if Kenny conceded. I had work, but I had no car so that I could only take a job if someone else in the area was also working and would give me a ride. I looked for a moderately priced used car ad finally brought one home to show Kenny. (I, as a wife, did not have the ability to purchase it in my name.) Kenny agreed that the car was a good buy but he refused to sign the contract. I returned the car. For three days I felt completely bound up by these circumstances as if my life was confined to a 1x1' square. I kept looking to God to resolve this impasse. On the third day, my brother Jim called to tell me that he was moving back to the Midwest. Did I want to take over payments on his Maverick? I resurrected all the way to San Francisco and drove home with the car.

Name your favorite hobby. When and where did you start doing it? Why do you enjoy it?

Genealogy. My Dad use to tell us that it is important to know one's roots and one's history is the source of much that can bring us both pride and humility. Pat began collecting data about our ancestors early on and I kept the oral history going. I had a huge store of memories of what had been and I had saved every letter I had ever received, as well as bits of memorabilia from bygone days. Occasionally Mother would say I wish I could find a record of my _____ (some obscure relative) and I began to help her search. Also, I became intrigued with the mass of information safely guarded by Pat. Before Dad died he set down a fairly complete record of his forebearers. I became hooked and I was very good at it. I had done a lot of research for John Sheppard. He always said that the ideal job for me would be researcher for a writer. I had done a lot of work that involved examining public records. I was good at finding sources based on scraps of information that Mom would drop from time to time. I developed the kind of family history that seemed important to me. One thing I learned is that the majority of people take interest in geneaology so late in life that those of their elders who might have given first-hand information about one's ancestors are already dead and gone.

What was the hardest thing you ever had to do?

Ask for money or financial assistance from another. I was always ashamed of being dependent on others despite my skills, my initiative, my industry. I had worked from my youth bought my clothes and my books and paid tuition all through high school. I had been a well paid employee of the hospital for seven years and a better paid employee at Western union. I was respected as a responsible employee. I was proud of my work record. All of that changed when Kenny decided that I should quit work. From then on I had no right to any money. All of my worldly goods came as the result of Kenny's largesse because all of the money in the house was his. I was very hurt by this attitude and having to negotiate for even the bare necessities. I felt used and exploited. No mater how hard I worked or how I scrimped and saved, I was not worthy of any compensation. When my teeth began to fall out, Kenny's response was, "I can't afford a dentist." This situation affected me deeply. I wavered between feeling I was a second-class citizen, a poor relation, a pitiable creature or that I had a serious flaw that I would not face.

Have you ever participated in a rally or demonstration?
What was the cause? What were your feelings about it?

In high school, there were the Pep Rallies and the boycott of Duel in the Sun, a demonstration in reverse. In the late fifties, anti-communism occasioned many rallies, speakers meetings and banquets honoring leaders of the movement. Than there were the packed meetings of the Magnolia School Board, to ensure a high standard for the curriculum and the educational tools that could be used. Larry and Kenny and I became involved in Republican Party politics and registered voters, walked precincts, manned polling places and attended all of the Central Committee meetings. In 1962, we all worked for the Republican Congressional candidate, Bob Geier, for whom we held coffees and acted a initiators of discussions of key issues at mass meetings, participated at all policy making and strategy meetings and handed out literature and discussed our candidates platform at rallies. I did fundraising for Bob and I solicited donations from O.C. professionals for $100 a plate dinner at Disneyland hotel at which Ronald Reagan, who had recently changed his affiliation to Republican, was the greatest speaker. I know the political scene very well. When John Kennedy won and all of our candidates lost, I was inspired to pray about it. My life was changed yet again.

Did the pastor or a visiting missionary ever come to your house for dinner or tea? Share on vivid experience.

Ah yes! Father McIntyre was our pastor at Christ the King Church in Haddonfield, NJ. My Daddy knew him well, but he didn't visit our home. The first priest who impressed me was a clergyman in another parish who was talking to Daddy as I stood by, I told Daddy that I needed to go to the bathroom and he asked the priest where it was. I didn't know what impressed me more—that this stranger, a priest, recognized my need and came to my aid or that there was a bathroom in church. Father Kelly, a Navy Chaplain, often came to dinner when we lived in San Diego. He was very handsome. At fourteen I noticed that sort of thing. He was also very natural (i.e. unaffected) in short sleeves drinking beer with Daddy and laughing with us over the family pictures especially one of Mom with her long shapely legs in stockings and tights which Jane pronounced was Mother when she was in burlesque. Then when the boys went to the seminary there was Beto, beloved Beto. I always felt a strong affinity with priests. It was as if with all of the variables considered—difference of expression politically, societally, philosophically—there was a bond between us that gave us the ability to relate to each other.

Did you ever go on a hayride or bob for apples? Tell about fun harvest activities you enjoyed with other young people.

We used to bob for apples at parties on Halloween. It was a messy game, even if one liked water and I didn't enjoy it very much. Hayrides are another story. There were several places in Paramount that rented hay wagons when I was in high school. Hayrides in those days were not the type of event portrayed in movies. There was usually singing and joking around and boisterous behavior. Making out was not accepted by most of the young people of my era. After graduation when I belonged to a young singles club called The Anthonians we sometimes went on hayrides. We would rent the hay wagon at Veorles on Carson right after the San Gabriel River bridge and their driver would takes us riding down country roads for a couple of hours. There was usually some beer and soda, singing and laughing. I met a very nice young man named Bob Wilcox on one of those hayrides. Bob was 25 and he had just returned form the Air Force. He was one of the finest men that I ever dated. He owned his own business with his father. We dated for several months. For Christmas, he gave me a complete set of Evening in Paris (about $25.00, a huge amount in those days.)

Where did your father go to work every day and what did he do?

I remember living in Florida where Daddy cared for an orange grove. We lived in Cocoa Beach miles down an oyster bed road far removed from our nearest neighbor. From the road we walked over a wooden bridge through the palmettos to an old wooden house with woodpecker holes in the roof and a screen door on which chameleons would climb. In the yard was a barrel for collecting rainwater. My Daddy killed a snake there once. Then I remember our Daddy pumping gas, selling Christmas cards, Avon products, and ice cream at football games. It was the depths of the Depression. When Daddy became a mailman, life improved economically. Daddy would tell us little bits of news that he learned from walking his route. While he had this job, Daddy began to consider being a Civil Service employee which affirmative decision led to his becoming a draftsman of Navy ships. Except for the times when he worked in the petroleum industry or as Inspector for the construction of the Long Beach Water Treatment Plant, Daddy went seaward. He grew to love the Navy and the ships and "The Laws of the Navy" from the Bluejackets Manual were frequently quoted.

Describer your father in his working clothes.

When I was a small child, men who worked in offices, regardless of their type of work or their position on the staff, dressed as professional men in the more formal attire of their day. Daddy wore a long sleeve white starched broadcloth shirt and a conservative tie over which was a vest that matched his suit. His suit was always clean and pressed and his oxford shoes were polished to a glossy shine. Hats were essential not only for a stylish appearance, but for protection from the elements. In the winter, Daddy's hat was felt with a medium brim and a crease down the middle of the crown. In the summer men wore Charlie hats. There were made of a coarse straw and they had a rigid brim about 2 ½" wide and a stiff flat crown. Or as an alternative there were Panama hats of soft closely woven pale fibers in the same design as the felt hat. In winter a top coat (to the top of the knee), but more commonly an overcoat completed the costume of the well-dressed man. My Daddy was always impeccably dressed. He was a handsome man with a slim figure (Larry most resembled him) who wore his clothes well.

Who in your family served in the military and when? Do you have a special memory of that person?

My Dad was a member of the National Guard for the State of Pennsylvania. He was appointed to West Point subject to passing the entrance examinations. Dad's father hired a tutor to help him prepare, but as Dad lamented late in life, he wasn't with the program. He failed the test and joined the Cavalry where he spent two enlistments. During the late thirties Dad developed a love for the U.S. Navy which never left him. The Navy, despite his knowledge and experiences, refused him a commission in World War II and he accepted a commission in the Coast Guard. Due to his knowledge and expertise he was sent to the Bureau of Ships in Washington, D.C. It was an awful experience which greatly disheartened my Dad and, when all other avenues failed to resolve matters, Dad resigned his commission. He enlisted in the Navy as an Apprentice Seaman, went through boot camp at San Diego and much to his chagrin served throughout the duration of the war on the Pacific Coast. Kenny served with the First Division of the U.S.M.C. in Korea and my brothers, Tom and Michael, served as career Navy personnel in the Viet Nam War.

What were your family finances like when you were growing up? How did that affect you?

As children we were never made aware of the desperate years of the Great Depression. Only in later years was I given to see some of the inconsistencies of my early childhood as stemming from the poverty of those years. The fact that we had a wood stove, kerosene lamps and that my mother and Mommom ironed with flat irons didn't seem strange. Our neighbors were not better off and further some conveniences which we now take for granted were only then coming into use. Refrigerators were only on the market since the 20's. More people still had ice boxes that kept food cold with a block of ice. My parents and grandparents felt fortunate for a roof over our heads, a garden and some little food besides some coal in the bin and good health. Despite a constant shortage of funds there was always a handout for the hobos who came to the door. Transients in search of work, hungry and often grubby begging for a little food were never turned away. My Daddy had a strong sense of responsibility as the wage earner of the family and he prided himself on never having gone on Relief.

What kind of car did your family drive? Were you proud of it or embarrassed by it? Why?

We had no car at all until I was eight years old. We lived on the outskirts of Camden across the Delaware River from metropolitan Philadelphia. There were buses to any area at frequent intervals. The automobile did not really come of age until after the war (WWII). And there was the Great Depression of the 1930's when people were so intent on having a job for the necessities of life that such a luxury as a car was pie in the sky. In 1938 we moved to Newport News, VA. and my Dad bought a 1934 Ford Sedan. It was green with a sloped back. Every night, with Larry peering over his shoulder from the back seat, my Daddy would race the freight train to Williamsburg. On Sundays we would travel to Catlet, VA. to see the Nurse family who lived on a huge horse farm that the family had owned since the Civil War or we would travel miles through rural Virginia (most of the state) to find a historical site. Sometimes we went to Yorktown or Buckarow Beach to swim. Highway 1 was under construction and my Dad often drove it to see what progress was being made. When we moved back to NJ the car was sold.

Did you ever feel that God had a special calling on your life?

When I was in high school I offered Mass every morning at 6:30 AM. It was still dark when I left the house at 5:45 AM. In the Winter we had thick fog in the morning. We lived in a neighborhood between two streets with houses scattered around at random for the space of a couple of blocks. I remember hoping that I was heading for the bus stop and hoping that when I put my hand out I wasn't going to touch someone else in the darkness. Nevertheless, even in pleasant weather when it was light in the morning I was of a mind to reach the Church and savor the bit of solitude that I found at Mass. One morning when the priest raised the body of Christ at the Consecration, instead of the priest, I saw myself offering Christ to the world. My first reaction was that I was fantasizing or that I had dozed off. The next morning the same message came to me and at night I dreamed over and over again of that moment when God seemed to speak to me. It was the mission that I was given and that I accepted. For several years I considered seriously becoming a religious, that is entering the sisterhood of the Immaculate Heart or Maryknoll, but such an expectation was unrealistic in that my deepest need was for a continuation of "family" as I knew it.

What favorite Christmas treasures have you kept from year to year? Share their origins.

In the Eastern part of the country a big event was a trip to the city to see the Christmas decorations. We went to Philadelphia five or six miles away and on the other side of the Delaware River. All of the big department stores seemed to compete with each other. Wanamaker's had a huge pipe organ on the ground floor and teams of employees singing Christmas carols around it throughout the day. One department was lit with blue lights and covered with artificial snow and scenes from the North Pole. It was so real that one even felt colder there. There was a huge room set up only for trains. You can't imagine how extensive those displays were. It was as if the toy Lionels were really traveling to all kinds of places. through tunnels in mountains, over bridges into towns with a Post Office, stores, churches, schools, houses and out into the countryside with houses, barns, silos, cows, horses, sheep, etc. and on to the station fully equipped with baggage wagons, a ticket office and depot. And after visiting all the stores, the wait in the snowy Plaza for the bus home. I remember being filled with the sights and sounds standing in the cold stamping my feet, clapping my hands to keep warm and always Mother and Daddy.

Describe your mother in her best dress.

My mother was always a stylish dresser. I remember particularly a black crepe dress (she was wearing it in the family group picture taken in front of the fireplace on Constitution Lane. It had padded soft shoulders and raglan cut short sleeves. The bodice was loosely fitted with a V neckline. It had a skirt eased onto the bodice that hung in a straight line to the knee. It was belted at the waist. Crepe is a luxurious fabric. My Mother had long shapely legs and excellent posture and she wore her hair in a short soft wave. She looked quite elegant to me. But I remember my Mother also in a Hoover Apron which was a popular wrap around dress in a cotton house dress such as all housewives wore in those days. Daddy sent her material for a dress from Hawaii, bright blue with white tropical flowers and I remember her in that dress. I also remember wedgies and I can still see them on my Mother's feet. Turbans were also in fashion in 1940 and my Mother wore one that was white. There is a snapshot somewhere taken on the beach at Maui of my Mother in a black bathing suit. She was in her eighties by that time but everyone who saw the picture guessed that she was twenty years younger.

How did your mother spend her day? Did she have a job or do volunteer work outside the home?

My mother and, in my early years, her mother with whom we lived were never still. In the morning when I woke up there was always the sounds of homemaking in progress. The soft clanging of pots on the woodstove, water running, clothes in our washer swishing or the sound of the rollers in the wringer squeezing out the excess water. When I awakened to these sounds I knew that all was well with the world and even as a child, I would luxuriate in my good fortune. Monday was washday and this chore was not the easy take it is today. The washer was filled with hot water and the clothes were agitated for the prescribed time. Then the stationary tub was filled with cold water and the clothes were run through the winger into this rinse. This process was repeated and then the clothes were attached to the clothesline with wooden pins and the lines were propped so that nothing could drag on the ground. The clothes before synthetic fabrics were fairly limp once they were washed and the sizing was gone. Bring on the starch! Steaming hot and slimy in a big pot on the stove. If this wasn't enough, there was the laborious task of ironing clothes with flat irons on the wood stove.

Share a memory of your grandparents or an older person you loved.

My Grandmother was a volatile person whose passion and energy were evident in everything she did. She was a large woman with brunette hair. Her complexion tended toward olive and she had beautiful brown eyes. To skinny me she seemed like a mama bear. She loved the "soap operas" especially "Aunt Jenny's Scrapbook". I can still picture her crocheting like a fury and perspiring over a kettle of doughnuts. I was fascinated at the drama of some "heated" arguments that she had with Daddy. He met his match in her and he never lost his respect for her. My Grandfather was a quiet, sober man with a kindly patient manner. I was his shadow as he cultivated his garden, hammered and sawed or shaped wood, or picked berries or polished his mallet. There was always room for me on his lap and I sat next to him at the table. When I was sick there were his home remedies like Goose Grease, Black Salve and Sulphur Powder for my sore throat. I remember sitting at his knee while he fed me slices of onion which I loved. In summer, he would walk me around the block for an ice cream cone with sprills. He was often in pain from a stomach ailment, but the only time he ever shushed me was when he was listening to baseball. Poppop taught me how to tie my shoe laces.

Tell about a memorable Christmas visit with relatives.

Mother and Dad were living in Bremerton, WA. Tom, Ruthie and Michael were in high school. It had been a busy year. I had been pregnant in a "big" way with John. During the summer, Rita had attempted suicide and Laura and Amy stayed at our house while she was recovering. It was a very hot summer. We had the inside of the house painted. I had no sooner gotten the house back in order and sent Rita and her little ones home when I delivered John. A mother later, I was hospitalized with an infected gall bladder and on December 1st I had it removed. The trip to Bremerton was undertaken so that we could spend Christmas with my parents. We had a very small Mercury and it snowed from Redding on, but the five kids were good travelers despite the cold and the cramped quarters. Kenny drove straight through and we arrived in Bremerton about 4 AM where I went to phone and called Dad for directions. He told us how to get to a certain station where he would meet me. As we drove up there he was in his Smoky the Bear costume. I can see him still. He was always there for me.

Share a family tradition or memory from the Fourth of July.

I remember awakening early in the morning to the popping of Cap Sticks. These were long red sticks with a piece of metal on one end and a slot for a cap. When the stick was pounded on the ground, the cap popped. July was hot in New Jersey and food was often picnic fare, but before ham, potato salad, sliced tomatoes and corn on the cob, was the Parade. Besides the American Flag proudly displayed on each house were the flags and bunting and crepe paper streamers on King's Highway, the main street. The Parade had the high school band, homemade floats, contingents of veterans from three wars (Civil War, Spanish America War and World War I) and adults and children on trikes, bikes, unicycles, in baby buggies all swathed in red, white and blue crepe paper. I proudly rode my tricycle. In the evening after dark, which only added to my enjoyment (the most exciting time of the day was night to my mind) there were the fireworks with the whoosh and hissing and the thunderous booming of spectacular pyrotechnics. I was especially impressed by the rocket and the displays rigged to show Uncle Sam and at the end of the show the American Flag. Then home to bed. It was one of my favorite holidays.

Have your even been in an accident, had surgery or a long illness? Tell me about it.

Even though I was a very skinny child who took in every contagious childhood disease that came up the pike (chicken pox, three different strains of measles, mumps, scarlet fever, whooping cough) I was in the main, healthy. All attempts to fatten me up or to boost my metabolism failed. Although I was always feeling weak and listless, I was so frightened by these symptoms that I early on developed the habit of keeping on the move. I fell downstairs when I was three, was bribed to have my nose packed and promptly pulled out the packing after I was paid off. About a year or so later, I lost my thumb nail due to my exploration of a revolving door at Sears. I didn't miss one day of school at St. Anthony in the four years of high school. In September 1949, I had an appendectomy. I delivered all of my seven children speedily easily without any anesthetic. Despite at least six miscarriages, doctors have been amazed at my excellent physical condition. I used to joke about having my uterus and cervix bronzed for all posterity. In 1964, I had my gall bladder removed. In 1974, I had a blood clot in the calf of my left leg. In 1998, I had a hematoma removed from my left lung. In 1999, I came close to losing my right thumb to squamous cell cancer and I have since had three more excised on my left arm and on each leg. I had two more in my thumb, have stenosis of the urethra and due to plaque in my artery, I have a subclavian stent.

Tell about your most memorable trip by plane, train or ship.

We traveled by train for the most part. It was still the transport of choice when I was young. It was thrilling to walk along the track beside the great iron engine hissing and letting off steam and to enter the luxury of the Pullman cars of those days. We traveled first class at government expense. On our first trip across country we had the entire car to ourselves except for Emily Hunt a New York debutante who kept us laughing throughout the trip. Jenny Dolly, one of the Dolly Sisters and an actress was also onboard. She took a liking for Pat who was terrified of her. We took the northern route and the scenery was spectacular. Dining was a whole new experience. The tables were covered with heavy starched linen tablecloths and on each was a bouquet of flowers, full settings of silver, china and fingerbowls and linen napkins . . . The food was ordered from a menu. When we returned to our car, our berths were made up for the night. I slept in a lower berth with a window. So I could lie in bed and look at the stars at night and in the morning I could view the snow-covered mountains. I enjoyed relating to new people in an environment that was also new—the porter, the conductor, the people we met—and observing the people who inhabited: different" regions of the country we passed through.

Describe a perfect summer day.

Pleasant coolness, soft breezes, swimming. Swimming was the most delightful part of summer and there was seldom the opportunity to swim until we went to Honolulu. There weren't even soft breezes or pleasant coolness until we moved to Santa Cruz. I believe that is the first place that we lived that I found summer enjoyable. Santa Cruz is on Monterey Bay and it extends up from the bay on the south and the cliffs on the west up into the foothills of the mountains. Before the college was built, it was a lovely peaceful small town. There were only about twenty children in my class and we were a close knit group. The movies cost 15 cents and entrance to the boardwalk was free. Even the part that had the roller coaster the roulette wheel (a ride where you sat as close to the center of a revolving floor and eventually flew onto a three story slide) had a very reasonable entrance fee. We spent hours on the boardwalk and at the beach with friends. There was camping in the mountains among the redwoods and weenie roasts with the Girl Scouts. I used to cut lawns for people in the neighborhood. I moved the lawn for a family who owned a woman's wear store downtown and earned the price of a bathing suit in their window. Summer was also the time that Mary Ellen Conrado and I would try to out read each other.

How old were you when you met Dad and what attracted you to him?

Twenty by three months—July 1949. Actually what attracted me to him was that he was attracted to me. I had seen him <u>once</u> speaking to others in the club, but I didn't know him. One night one of the girls who was recruiting people for the bowling team persuaded me to give it a try. I had never been in a bowling alley and I knew nothing of the game. Kenny was on the team where I was assigned. After bowling Kenny walked with me to the bus stop. While we waited, he covered a lot of ground conversationally. At one point he asked me. "What would you do if you had a baby and you weren't married?" A real show stopper and even a little scary considering that we were alone on an otherwise deserted corner in Belmont Shore at 10 PM. Kenny did not explain himself and his quandary about Judy and what was happening//since Verna had become pregnant and could no longer care for her. We took the Broadway bus to Atlantic and walked to Kenny's at 9th and Linden where I was introduced to the 1932 Chevrolet Sedan which had carried Willard (Doris' father), Eddie (her brother), Neal Fusco (a friend) and Kenny from Massachusetts to California. Kenny drove me home.

Share a memory about the way he proposed to you.

July 14, 1949 a summer night about 9 PM and Kenny and I were walking on the beach. I don't remember the conversation that might have inspired Kenny. We had been dating steadily from early May and we communicated well. (Lack of communication was never our problem.) Nevertheless, it took me by surprise when Kenny asked me to marry him. Contrary to the literature on the fantasies of young women I had never set my cap for a man, imagined the knight in shining armor who would sweep me off my feet or contemplated my wedding. My surprise stemmed from the fact of my devotion to Kenny, my attention to Kenny and our ability to relate to each other had taken us so easily to this pint,. I said yes, but that Kenny would have to ask my Dad. I went home and told my Mother. Her response was, "Don't be foolish. You have to get up early. You better get to bed." The next Sunday evening Kenny arrived to ask my Dad for my hand. Dad had had a few drinks. His response to Kenny was, "Don't try to take advantage of me when I've been drinking. Come back Wednesday night." Dad's reservation was that he didn't know Kenny's family or their values. And there were also Louis Dauer and Mac Cassidy who kept showing up unannounced when I was out with Kenny. They were both sailors whom I dated and Dad was taken with them. Or was he just stuck on the uniform?

Tell me about your wedding day, from beginning to end.

I am certain that I bathed and performed the usual steps to getting dressed without any assistance, but my first memory is of my sister Pat and I standing before a mirror doing our hair.

I had curly hair and I had gone to have it set at the beauty salon. On that morning, I was displeased with the results. So about half an hour before we left for the Church, I washed it and combed it as I liked it. Pat was a nervous wreck and trembling as we stood in the vestibule and Daddy covered his emotion by "letting off steam" (hissing through his teeth). Ruthie, age 1 year and 7 months looked adorable as my flower girl and she provided relief from tension as my flower girl by dumping all of her flowers at once. Larry and Jimmy were the altar boys and Tommy was my ring bearer. Jane was my first bridesmaid and Pat was my maid of honor. Pat was up on all of the etiquette involved, but I was used to following what seemed to me common sense. I don't think that there was a noticeable faux pas. Kenny's sister, Marlene, had recently moved to California and she was a bridesmaid. Also the wedding on Ascension Thursday drew a full Church. The reception was in the Church hall after which Kenny and I departed to our apartment and then our honeymoon. St. Lucy Church, Long Beach, California May 18, 1950.

What did you wear on your wedding day?

My wedding dress was made of frosted organdy (i.e. a fabric with a flowered white, overall flowered pattern on a background of white organdy) over a taffeta slip. It was a floor length princess style with a pointed stand up collar and long fitted sleeves. Kenny's Aunt Ruth made my gown for $14.00 and the materials cost me less than $20.00. My veil was a fingertip length of tulle which I sewed onto a pearl crescent-shaped tiara. On the day before the wedding, I purchased a pair of white leather flats with a single strap across the instep for $2.98. I had not, contrary to reports on the things young girls dream about, ever contemplated a wedding and definitely not mine. If I had thought at all of the event by which I would make the transition from single to married, it was in the months that immediately preceded the wedding. My thinking that a small private ceremony at 6:30 AM Mass with the family and a few friends in attendance would suffice changed due to my Mother's desire that I have a bridal gown and attendees and all of the trappings of a proper wedding which my parents elopement had denied her. Thus spoke my Father and I cancelled.

Where did you go on your honeymoon? Share one humorous incident.

Santa Cruz, California. We didn't own a car. Our transportation was a 1937 Indian straight four motorcycle. It didn't have a buddy seat. Kenny built a raised seat and two large compartments for luggage on either sided of the rear wheel. We traveled up Hwy. 101 along the coast and nearly froze even at the end of May. Our destination, Brookdale Lodge, was in Felton in the mountains. Our cabin was poolside. The dining room was built on tiers on either side of the brook. On Friday night we started out for Stagnaro's, a popular fish restaurant on the pier in Santa Cruz, but the bike threw a hose which was finally replaced about 11:30 PM. The only place open was a posh restaurant having a grand opening, hardly the setting for bikers. It rained most of the way down the coast, a cold, cold rain; the trucks rocked us continuously and there were no facilities. My bladder was in a knot when we reached Santa Monica because only Kenny could step off the road to relieve himself. I was not permitted for several good reasons. Only one of the incidents of control which became the norm. But I was such a handy girl and definitely a good sport.

What was your first house or apartment together like?

When we married we rented a furnished apartment at 1296 Cedar in Long Beach. It had a living room, kitchen, bath and dressing room and, that fixture of a time long past, a Murphy bed. A Murphy bed is one that is hung on a wall within a closet and folds down and becomes an ordinary bed. The dressing room off the bath had a built in dressing table and large mirror and there was ample closets for clothes and storage as well as a built in chest of drawers. The living room was a large rectangle with two large windows on the north wall. We were on the top floor and the whole apartment was bright and sunny. The furniture was dark mahogany upholstered in a muted blue and gold. There was wall to wall carpeting, but I don't remember the color. The kitchen was a long narrow room with white appliances and counter tops of white tile. At one end there was a table and two chairs and at the other a door that opened on the hall and the stairway. Our first guests were Mother and Daddy. I don't remember what I cooked for dinner, but I baked my first apple pie for desert. We lived in this apartment for only two and a half months before Kenny was called by the Marine Corps to go to Korea.

When and where did you buy your first house? Describe the house and explain any significance it held for you.

Kenny returned home from Korea and was discharged. Daddy had taken half of his garage and had built a room for us. So we were staying there, free room and board, until Kenny found work. One Sunday Kenny and I left Doris with Mom and Dad and went looking for a place of our own to rent. It was evening when we saw a sign in front of some model homes advertising "No down to Veterans." Before we knew it we had purchased our first home at 3522 Stevely Street, Long Beach, CA. We were both surprised at our good fortune and thrilled. Mom and Dad were in their mid-forties when they purchased their first home and they were very impressed. The house had a 16'x16' square living room and a dining room that was about 10'x12', a long narrow kitchen with white steel cabinets about 7'high lining one wall, a service porch with a stationary tub and space for a washing machine, one bathroom with a tiled shower and tub and two ample bedrooms. There were ¾" thick oak floors and a large window in the dining room overlooking the front porch and an attached two car garage. We went every night to survey the progress from start to finish.

Who was your best friend after you were married?
Describe some of the fun things you did together.

Isobel came into my life when I lived on Lakewood Boulevard in Long Beach after Kenny was discharged. I was working for Western Union at the time, but I was on strike. On one morning while I was hanging clothes, Isobel came out and struck up a conversation. She lived in the apartment next door and she had two little boys, Martin and Lyle. Isobel invited me in for coffee and to see her Hidden Treasure bras that she had just purchased. We hit it off at once. We both liked to read, to laugh and to cook. We shared our frustrations with life, with husbands, with money, with our figures. Isobel taught me how to bake bread. We read all of Armour's books and Betty McDonald's, Peter Deveries, Robert Paul Smith's laughing all the way. After naps on Friday afternoon, she would come in with Lyle on her hip and a bottle of wine under her shirt. We discussed great ideas less for the point of reaching a conclusion than for the need to exercise our brains. When we moved into our home and I became pregnant and I began having problems, I was bed ridden. Isobel would walk those three miles each way pulling Lyle in his wagon to care for me. We came to be a foursome and we enjoyed many memorable adventures. I credit Isobel as the one who revealed to me that life is not just black and white.

What kind of outdoor activity do you like? Why?

I enjoy digging in the dirt and planting, weeding, watering and pruning. In this, I must remember my grandfather who always had a garden stamped in my brain in the sight of bright red radishes being pulled from the black soil by Poppop. Gardens were more common when I was a child. Peas, tomatoes, radishes, green beans were common crops and old fashioned flowers like hollyhock, morning glory, flags, irises, sweet peas, pinks and lily of the valley seemed to rise unbidden in the nooks and crannies of our backyard. Tea roses were a favorite and in summer we would pluck off the shiny Japanese beetles that attached themselves to them and mix them with cold squishy mud to have mud pies with "raisins". The absolute queen of the garden was the lilac, but not only because of its color and luxuriant blossoms, but also because of the pungent odor. I like a lot to walk in residential neighborhoods, to observe the people, to see something of their concept of home. I enjoy being in the thick of things rubbing shoulders with the crowd on Main Street, at the theater, anywhere that I can discern purposeful activity. I love being a part of churning humanity but yes, I do hate mob scenes and spectacular exhibitions.

Record here some gardening or decorating tips that you have found helpful:

When the family was still functional gardening was the ordinary pastime for the whole family every Saturday. However, in the days of my childhood Poppop was the gardener. He seemed to know, by instinct, how and when to plant and prune and reap the fruits of his labor. It was Mother not Daddy who cared for our yard and garden. She loved to be out digging in the dirt, cutting and watering in her barefeet. Daddy used to say that she was shaming him in front of the neighbors, but it was a joke. He was always fascinated by people who could work with their hands (a little envious too, I think, because his talents didn't run in that direction.) Mother could put a stick in the ground and it would flourish.

Share your favorite dessert recipe:

I don't have one? I have made many desserts though so I will say something about them. When Kenny was in Korea I used a Tomato Soup Cake recipe and substituted pureed persimmons for the soup. The finished product went overseas in coffee cans. There was a cake I made that was chocolate batter poured over a base of brown sugar butter and pecans. When it was turned out the brown sugar/pecan was the topping. I used up over ripe bananas (a rarity) by pureeing them and using them as a substitute for that much liquid in a yellow cake recipe. With walnuts added the result was a very good banana cake. Larry's favorite was Pineapple Upside-Down Cake and I have made my share of these as well as Lemon Meringue pie which Kenny preferred over cake.

Describe your personal style in clothing, make up or skin care, and hair care:

I have always loved dressing up which not only enhanced my natural attributes but also gave me a boost of energy. I stood straight in heels and I was more conscious of how I appeared to others. I have been always intent on showing order and beauty through color and texture and choosing for my attire what was appropriate for the occasion. I have never cared for makeup possibly because I don't like the feeling of facials and the cream on my face put me in a panic of breathlessness. My hair has always been low maintenance. I had naturally curly hair from the time I was seven until I was sixteen. I never had a haircut and it was very, very long. From sixteen on I have worn it short. I could cut it, wash it and comb it and be on my way in half an hour.

Share a favorite Thanksgiving or Christmas recipe:

Gather together the whole family and all of your close friends under one roof. Send one of the male adults to the nearest military base to pick up a couple of servicemen with no place to go.

While the turkey is roasting, set up the tubs and dish drainers in the garage. As people arrive greet them, offer them a drink of their choice. Be sure there is music for added cheer. Mother will come and the second turkey with her. Start to carve the turkey keeping an eye out for Larry who likes to sneak little bits of it off the platter. Don't forget the gravy. Agree good humouredly with Dad's "suggestions". Usher everyone to the tables. Say the blessing and eat.

After dinner relax as the young people clear the tables and leave to wash the dishes. Turn up the music try to talk over John Philip Sousa and laugh a lot at the good fortune of family.

Share a favorite poem or a passage of writing that has been especially meaningful in your life.

A Bag of Tools

Isn't it strange
That princes and kings
And clowns that caper
In sawdust rings
And common people
Like you and me
Are builders for eternity?

Each is given a bag of tools,
A shapeless mass,
A book of rules;
And each must make—
Ere life is flown—
A stumbling block
Or a stepping stone

R.L. Sharpe

If not my favorite, often remembered when I am
inclined to bemoan a difficult crisis.